Confessions:
Brainstormin' from Midnight 'til Dawn

C. Liegh McInnis

Psychedelic Literature/Jackson, Mississippi

Psychedelic Literature ®

203 Lynn Lane
Clinton, MS 39056
(601) 383-0024
psychedeliclit@bellsouth.net

Copyright © 1998, 2007 by C. Liegh McInnis for Psychedelic Literature. All Rights Reserved, including the right of reproduction in whole or in part in any form without permission in writing from the author.

LCCN: 98-091295
ISBN: (13 digit) 978-0-9655775-2-6
ISBN: (10 digit) 0-9655775-2-X

Other Works by C. Liegh McInnis
Matters of Reality: Body, Mind, & Soul (Poetry, 1996)
The Lyrics of Prince (Lyrical Criticism, 1997)
Scripts: Sketches and Tales of Urban MS (Fiction, 1998)
Searchin' for Psychedelica (Poetry, 1999)
Prose: Essays and Letters (Social Commentary, 1999)
Da Black Book of Linguistic Liberation (Poetry, 2002)
Poetic Discussions (Interviews, DVD 2005)
Introduction of a Blues Poet (Poetry, CD 2005)

Acknowledgements

To the Creator: Thank you for keeping me safe in your love while [i] wandered through the wilderness of my will. [i] know now that all blessing come from you, and [i] can do all things through you. Glorihighlove!

To Monica: (Soul of my Soul) My female reflection. [i] am nothing without you. Joy remains; for everyday is another day to fall in love with you. There is no time, only us and God. Peace baby.

To Joshua P.: You are infinitely wiser than [i] will ever be. The world is yours if your prepare yourself.

To Natasha T. Pain and anger are evils with which we all must do battle. You must control them and not let them control you. No matter your past, only you control your future. What you will write in the heart of time?

To C. Liegh Sr.: Thank you for demanding more. [i] love you.

To Claudette M. (Mama) Thank you for the unconditional love. [i] love you.

To the McInnis-Winfield Extended Family: Foundation is the most important element in a child's life. Thank you all.

To the Birdland Poets: Thanks for teaching me a new trick.

To David Brian Williams: Every time you share an image, you make me want to get better. Thanks for keeping the soul in the work.

To Jolivette Anderson (The Poet Warrior): Candles and incense, honey and chocolate, you are the Dawn's morning Sun. Keep raining down your revolution.

To Derrick Johnson: Economics and Art is a circular relationship. Keep telling our children this.

To Kamelia (Queen): Black beauty is a metaphysical thing. Your waters run deep, girl.

To Rhonda Richmond: Your voice is like an Angel. My soul climaxes when you sing.

To Nellie Mac: You keep causing me cardiac liberation. Your bass reminds me [i] am alive.

To Rufus Mapp: Upon this beat [i] build my funk. Through your hand my soul can feel my African connection.

To Ezra and Terry: Horns Galore!!! Saxophone and Trumpet on the one!!! Too Nasty!!!

To Brown River Production: Artistic souls find each other.

To Diallo. Thanks for the support when [i] needed it most.

To Uganda: The Delta is the soul of the world. Your lines tell us this.

To Uzoma and the Path to Freedom: Thanks for looking out for the children.

To Colleen W.: One day all of us will find our "Dwelling Place."

To Rhondalyn: Every month is woman's month. Thank you for teaching this.

To West Jackson: [i] wouldn't be anywhere else.

To the JSU English Department: Thanks for the tolerance and the education. Our diversity is our beauty.

To Dr. Inez Morris: Thanks for taking a chance on me.

To Dr. Marie O'Banner-Jackson: Thank you for the sanity, the peace, and letting me be a brat.

To Kenny Patterson: Your kind soul is proof of God's angels.

To Tyrone, Will, and Jackie: Body and Soul. [i] can never thank you guys enough.

To Angela R.: Your love for words make it a joy to come to work.

To Dr. Wanda Macon: Clarksdale in the house. Thanks for keeping it real even when real is unpopular.

And to you: Thanks for allowing me to share myself with you. [i] hope you get something that you can use. Peace, Rain and Sunshine…Rainbows forever. See you in the Psychedelica.

Table of Contents

	Epigraph	7
I.	Preface	8
II.	Introduction	11
	Confession	12
	To God	14
III.	Regrets, Pain, and Sorrows	16
	Hawthorn's Blithedale	17
	Revolution of One	18
	Do My Fat Body a Favor	20
	Empty Orgasms (Sexing to Survive)	21
	The Mirror	24
	Lowell's Beethoven	25
IV.	Memory	26
	The Coz on the *Tonight Show*	27
	The Smell of You on my Pillow	29
	Pecola's Dance	31
	Daydreaming of a Wife on the Pascagoula Beach	32
	Birdland's Angels	34
	A Girl Named Chris	36
V.	Anxiety	38
	A Poet not by Choice	39
	To You	41
	[i] Hate Christmas	43
	To the Musician	45
	Hold on to Your Insanity	46
	The Unrequited Calling (for Jonah, Moses, Medgar, and Martin)	48
VI.	Love(?)	50
	The Beat of My Love	51
	You Are Sex	52
	The Reading of the Kiss	55

	Everyday Is another Day to Fall in Love with You	57
VII.	Concerns	58
	Where Is the Temple of my Familiar?	59
	To Be Post-Colonial Isn't to Be Re-indigenous(?)	61
	Letter to the Northern Negro	63
	God Has a Napoleon Complex	65
	Tripping on my One	67
	Open Letter to a College Professor	69
VIII.	Suicide Note	71
IX.	Reconciliation	75
	Am [i] a Hypocrite?	76
	To Joshua and Natasha	78
	Repentance: A Sinner's Prayer	79
	Hair Complex	81
	Exercise in Identity	83
	Friendship	84
	The Lord's Prayer, 1998	85
X.	Dreams, Visions, and Epiphanies	86
	Dream Catcher	87
	Pieces of Heaven	88
	Regeneration	90
	Ghetto Garden	91
	Revolution is Born from Pain	93
	My Psalm	95

Epigraph

It isn't the teeth of death that frighten me frigid,
but the manner in which the uncertainty of an afterlife
pushes me around like a playground bully.

Preface

3:18 in the a.m., and my mind won't stop tumbling.
Outside my window birds doze,
but the video playback in my head's cinema rolls on.
Blurred pictures of January and July run through my body;
a clammy finger rubs against my
humid and sticky emotions.
Now [i] lay me down to sleep,
but [i] seem to have missed the bus.
The paint splattering montage of wrestling colors
keeps raging swirling blues that shank olive dreams.
Spring suffers from multiple sclerosis.
Quick and sharp strokes of red,
the forest fires in my head burn the retaining wall that
separates wishes from will do, as dashes of growling greens
and yelling yellows pour sweaty ashes into my bed.
A man's bionic voice is the uninterested narrator
of my dime store soap opera of nights.
Prose and verse, fact and fiction, intermingle
like lint on poorly washed clothes as my ability
to perceive blurs the sandy edges of my mind's coast.
Thus, the only reality [i] now know is Poetica,
and she is a wayward trope who sleeps with me at her will.

My memories are random snow flakes melting before
hitting the jalapeno pavement of my conscience: a tingling
burned wrist, the electrical surge of the pain ran from my
wrist to my elbow and through the tips of my fingers.
Since then that hand holds things differently than the other,
like a scorched lover afraid to love.
…the first time [i] told a girl [i] liked her, her face was
granite with a long straight line chiseled across for a mouth,
two round eyes like lights on a train.
The train is coming; the car always loses.
She cared as much for my love as she cared for the slugs
that slide beneath the undersides of the church.
It wasn't her fault that she was beautiful.
Life is a lottery ticket that she had clearly won.
It was my twelve year old confession

that it took my tied tongue all summer to say,
words held like fine fragile china
cradled in the bubble wrap of my mind,
only opened and released with the last flower of summer
to the cold wind of her indifference.
That train just keeps coming.
With a sigh drenched with wet wretched rejection,
saying "So, what?"
[i] was seventeen before [i] asked a female to dance.
She sighed.

[i] remember striking out five times in one game.
Each and every swing, all fifteen, unique in their
varying manner in which they narrowly missed the ball—
an inch and a mile is all relative.
Each grunt and sigh with its own version of hot shame.
The pitcher smiling a cat's grin from ear to ear.
The catcher's mouth spewing with shit talking.
The adult umpire teaches life lessons that stick
with you like gum to the bottom of your psyche,
 "Come on kid, let's get this over with."
By the fourth at bat, your arms are tired,
not from swinging but from carrying
your heavy sandbags of embarrassment.
A Mississippi summer is a magnifying glass,
and the heat scorches you like a bug.
The fourth trip to the plate,
a pony tail cute girl with bright braces amuses,
"Here he comes again."
The crowd roars with laughter,
becoming a sea of pearly whites and tonsils.
After the fourth strikeout, the bench is four times as far.
Who keeps moving that damn bench?

[i] remember…

Shit…is the light bill paid…
the light bill is a humped back whale
docked on the sands of fear…
[i] mean will it be paid next month?

How about the cars?
(twin trouble tearing like termites the paper from my
pockets) Damn, is this room cold?
My scrotum seeks sanctuary in the cave of my stomach.

The last time [i] got some
is a memory wafting like a bird's evening chirp.
The last time [i] didn't perform well
is a memory piercing like a fire engine's siren
with flashing lights and blaring horn.
My face flush with ignited ignominy.
Lying there board stiff, she sighs.
"Sorry ass, anorexic dick muthafucker!"
"If the muthafucker couldn't fuck,
he shudda said so!"
She sighed again—
every sigh making my essence smaller than my penis.
Mountains, valleys, and oceans worth
of dispensing pleasure,
and [i] remember, most, when [i] clocked out early.
It's like thousands of stick pins pricking my soul.
So, she revokes my man card
due to my insufficient funds of testosterone.

So, is it absentee manhood that holds my eyelids up?
Can you be a man if you have no penis place?
How do you teach little Black babies
when you don't pollinate the curriculum?
It's handed down to you from pallid men who received
their dicks from the Constitution.
So, they have always been the cultural fornicators,
and a three-fifth citizen who wishes to flower
must unscrew his myth and become
a bitch's concubine, gelded and impotent,
unable to plant the seeds of life in his community.

What keeps you up nights??????????????????????????

Introduction

Confession

The red carpet to my honesty has been rolled out and is waiting for you. Come closer. Don't be afraid. It's only your mind. No one else is here but us. So, maybe we can be free to unlock doors that have been chained shut by our mortification that has hidden the key in the bosom of reason. If you are not afraid to be as curious as the cat, [i]'ve got something for your intuitive, which is engraved in your soul. Don't worry; it was what was in the garbage can, not the curiosity, that killed the seeker. If you want Truth as it relates to fact, [i] can only show you where [i] live. If you can put away your pregnant prejudices formed by your television enhanced memories and deal with what happens before the lights come on, [i] may say something to improve the flow of your philosophy's intestines. The freshly wrapped tomorrow makes meaning of eaten actions we digested from yesterday's meal. But this is not about some arm chair critic's deconstructed theme but more about the need of weary writers to play. Come on and order your world.

Confession, don't be afraid for your soul;
from time to time we all must inventory our shop's supply.
Confession, it's only good for the soul
when used to realign your inner ear symmetry.
Confession, checking your soul's medical chart
to see how heart healthy your life is.
Confession is understanding that the sandcastle
you build does not exist for eternity.

It's the constant cycle of rotating the tires of your mind
and always coding your tongue with sun-flavored Truth
'cause confession is the best gift that you can unwrap.
Confession, the ones smothering your shadow and the ones afraid to turn on the light in the cave are worried that the sharp arrows of your words will hit the bull's eye of their bullshit.
Confession, the second-hand sale of Truth is always negotiable to cover the rent and other notes you pay.

Confession emancipates you
from the slavery of dishonesty,
covering you with the liberating light of integrity.
Confession is the Noxzema that cleanses the ills, fears,
blotches, boils, and anxiety of a dirty and deceitful soul,
purging yourself of the weight of shame
to fly falcon free again.
Who you are lies in the womb of who you want to be
and understanding that the stick house "you"
that you build does not exist for an eternity.

It's a country tent revival that allows you to re-baptize
your principles into the cooling water of Truth
'cause confession is a pardon that only you can give to you.
Confession, realizing that you did not petition
the court of Nature to be here,
while normality's soldiers wonder why you won't adhere
to the sliding rules which they hold so dear.
Confession reduces fear to a direction instead of a compass,
knowing that your soul is being purified by crystal tears.
Confession is to rap to God when you check yourself,
questioning your poem before you critique God's novel.
Confession, the Magnolia-tall tantamount Truth,
means to sleep nights after the cleansing of your mind's
bowels.

To God

Guilt is a gnome in spiked shoes
tap-dancing on my chest.
My past is a dirty diaper
super-glued to my conscience.
My life is a pair of defiled draws,
and I have no coins for the Laundromat.
I hate niggas because they smell like me.
I'm the glutton who ate the green plumbs,
and then defecated on the blooming flowers.
And, I hate You…because
my index finger can't find truth's bull's-eye.

I fill my pockets before I feel my heart.
My second head has a larger brain than my first.
I'll fornicate with mud and wonder
why I ejaculate soot.
I love to make left turns,
but hate going in circles.
It's me, it's me, it's me oh Lord,
standing in the need of a good ass kicking
'cause spoiled seeds ain't nothing but
weeds waiting on the Gardner to turn his back.
And I hate You…because the house
built on my deeds has foundation problems.

If parenting skills were seeds,
I'd have no grass in my yard.
And if love were money,
I'd have to file for bankruptcy.
My love affair with myself has been
an act of masturbation that has left me dry.
Too many times have I put my plug into
sockets that don't belong to me and been
surprised when it shocked the shit out of me.
Is the *Bible* a condom for the soul?
And I hate You…because
I continued to kiss frogs
even after the warts had formed.

I've tried sweeping my past under the carpet
or discarding it like Tuesday's trash,
but the mailman of my memory continues
to put it back in my mind's mailbox.
I need to vomit, but I don't want to stain
my new satin shirt that's two sizes too small.
And if I tell the truth
will my imaginary friends still play with me?
Cement walls and iron bars don't hurt as much as
eyes caging my body with looks of disappointment.
And I hate You…because
the soufflé of my manhood has failed to rise.

Telling the truth can be like pulling up the carpet,
and I don't think that there are hardwood floors
beneath my life of shaggy lies.
Can I stop this hamster's wheel?
Shame keeps me running in circles.
Tomorrow and tomorrow and tomorrow…
my head still hurts while my feet are
nailed to the floor of my past.
Just once could You reach down into my throat
and pull out the lie that is clogging my colon?
And I hate You…
for giving me the car of my dreams.

I have a DUI for driving under the influence
of my own will,
and as the highway angels pull me over
I curse Your name
even though I poured the drink.
Once strawberry sweet will is now
salty vinegar that closes my windpipe
and suffocates me on my own desire.
I remain a man's body trapped in a child's pajamas—
a boy whose spiritual puberty never blossomed,
choking on the phallus of my own selfishness.

Regrets, Pains, and Sorrows

Hawthorne's Blithedale

Where is my Blithedale?
Born too far removed from Egypt's Harlem,
there is no Gilded Age for my people.
So, how can [i] geogrophize my Blithedale?
[i] came, following your pale paths and was led astray.

Can [i] find my culture's cradle between
Zenobia's androgyny or beneath Priscilla's veil?
As a poet, [i] watch, masturbating over my observations.
Yet, no Blithedale found in my napkins.

Power to the People! Black fists pumping,
anxiously penetrating the Neilson's white hearts.
But there is no Blithedale.

Black Panther Blithedale?
Killed by the insatiable stomach of its ambition.
The Negro's communist Blithedale?
Langston's disillusioned dream.
And Angela Davis went to jail. Is that Blithedale?

For my nappy headed, afro wearing brother and
my hands-on-her-hip chocolate Zenobia,
Blithedale is a bounced check marked insufficient funds.
Our Brook Farm went up in smoke and the remains
auctioned on integration's block in exchange for the
high-rise development of the Talented Tenth.
The slave's wish of Blithedale buried beneath a pile
of governmental benefits and broken promises.

Revolution of One

[i]'m locked away behind the
cream padded walls of my mind,
behind the asylum of my computer,
Joker-laughing at those who laugh at me.
This is my line-drawn-in-the-sand stand: to be singular.
This is my one-man-play revolution: to be divorced.
[i] want to write flaming fires about Liberation.
[i] want my words to be like
freely flowing waters and lazar straight arrows
that pinpoint shifting bleached stolen legacies
and malicious mis-education.
[i] want to spit acid words as prophetically profound as
"Black Art," "For Saundra," and "Stranger in the Village."
[i] want to stick my erect middle finger
in the indignant, down-the-nose face of America
and condemn her for her whoremongering ways.
But when [i] raise my heavy head
and open my lock-jawed mouth,
all that comes out is "Leave me alone,"
falling like discarded crumbs to the floor.
My numbed ass is tired and sore from sitting in meetings
that yield less progress than street corner begging.
My feet bark like starved dogs, red and burning,
from marching on vacant lot streets that lead
to the Capitol Building on a Saturday when no one's home
but the slaves cleaning the chambers.
[i] have head nausea from the same repetitive,
circular conversation of a dog chasing its tail
masquerading as civil rights dialogue.
My ears are stale bagels from hearing King's words
circumcised and pasted onto bumper stickers because
we never realized that the bullet that took him
was aimed at the plump hearts of organized labor.
Yet, when [i] pry open my mouth, wired with apathy,
all that comes out is "Leave me alone," exploding
into a dry power that evaporates before it's heard.
Leave me alone with your
breast-milk heavy organizations

and counterfeit institutions.
We all merely return to our pork eating,
Metrocenter Mall spending lives
when our camera close-up is over.
You can't build a strong chain with weak links.
Sovereign soldiers, not mindless masses,
are the feet of revolution.
So, until you are ready to write a recipe that teaches
clumps of controlled clay how to be individuals,
leave me alone.

Do My Fat Body a Favor

Just once, [i] want to be the sexual sandwich
that your legs long to embrace with your lower lips.
Just once, [i] wanna feel a pair of flaming eyes
as they peruse the highway and back roads of my body.
[i] know that this sphere is a lot to navigate,
but [i]'m willing to wait for you
to take roadside breaks along the way.

[i]'m tired of burying my love in the dark.
[i] wanna hang a neon ceiling sign to see
how your face contorts when you scream.
[i]'m tired of climbing into bed half camouflaged,
waiting until [i]'m under the cover to relinquish the rest.

Just once, [i] wanna be touched
by fingers that ache like lost lovers to feel me.
[i] wanna feel your hands attempting
to find Waldo in the haystack of my fields.
Just once, touch me like your favorite dress on sale.

With the moonlight spotlighting my body,
[i] want you to trace the frame of my steady shell.
[i] want you to turtle walk your lazy fingers
down the center of my heart's shield
and around my bulging love handles,
holding on like a bull rider for dear life.

Do my fat body a favor.
With your hands, savor me like hot soup on a winter's eve.
Caress me in places that [i] haven't seen in years.
And when it's over, hold me
like a dream from which you never want to wake
as if my bloated body is asylum of our fantasy.

Will you do me this one favor?

Empty Orgasms (Sexing to Survive)

When [i]'m finished, there's a lifeless pool,
where fish swim into emotional traps and die.
Sex without the soul is solitary and cold,
nothing more than two people masturbating together.
[i]'m an engine with no fuel,
a structure with no Jesus to make it a church.
When [i]'m in my woman,
her detached skin is all that [i] feel.
Moments after [i] release, [i]'m back to the real.
Her touch only finds my fleshly foreshadow.
Her soul's outlet finds no plug to fill her socket.
It bounces off my rubber casing and returns to her
stamped address unknown.
Her moaning calls to my inner phone go unanswered.
Two empty frames in a meaningless dance,
clanging entities making loud noises signifying nothing.

These are all nowhere nights, looking for a narcissistic
end to my constant stream of nothingness.
[i] undo two of her buttons, looking for heaven,
abandoned shacks fit only for transient inhabitants,
two cardboard cutouts trying not to be bored.
Just another night of labor at the same old job.
Just another female that [i] got to know from the back.
Try as [i] might, [i] cannot hump my way to inner peace.
[i] can't save my soul with some head and 69.
Sex becomes a magazine you read
while waiting for bad news in the doctor's office.
Writing dulls the pain as it cuts open the pores
to relieve the waste of myself. (Brain orgasm)
[i] eat late into the night,
forcing the flavor to produce fluids
titillating my tongue's erogenous zones.
Everything is better with food.
[i] am in a gluttonous utopia until [i] awake
three pounds larger;
sexual recreation is a soothing hobby
until a stomach grows.

Still, [i] sex lots of women because colonization is fun.
Call my name damit; let the world (or our neighbors)
know that Kilroy's darkened brother was here.
(No, you can't spend the night.)

My snapping turtle touch has no tenderness;
there is no sharing in my kiss.
[i]'m a man who thinks a slap on the ass is a caress.
My idea of foreplay is getting undressed.
My subway bed is crowed with sticky memories
from taking the world to sleep with me.
Closing my eyes only shows me
neon photographed negatives of pain and puberty.
My women, half-finished cross-word puzzles,
are just something to do,
only a narcotic for the night to help me get through.
Submission is the only wedding gift worth having.
[i] dominate her 'cause she's all that [i] can.
[i]'m just stabbing away my daily pains
instead of seeding new life with my woman.
When [i] roll over like a drunk after a binge,
[i]'m almost surprise to see her there.
The only way that [i] notice my woman
is when she is bare.
[i] still can't tell you how she wears her hair.

Sex is a sedative, some knock-me-out juice for the night,
getting off on the violence of pinning her down and
stabbing her repeatedly until she screams my name
like a bad actress in a "B" movie,
this false acknowledgement the only Oscar [i]'ll ever win.
This is the one sure way of planting the flag of my
manhood into her landscape annexed for my ego.
First [i] pillage and plunder, then [i] hack and sack.
My thrusts imitate the throbs of my aching head.
Since [i]'m Bigger Thomas' baby boy,
don't know if her screams of pleasure or pain
give me more joy.
It's the power of penetration that reaffirms that [i]'m alive.
So insecure, [i] never let her on top.

In bed, all positions of power are reserved for me.
For [i] can only exist through the power tool of my penis.
All day long, [i]'ve been the company's concubine.
That's why when [i] get home, [i]'m trying
to knock the bottom out of her elevated esteem.
Thick globs of sweat popping off my head and back,
baptize her in my swine.
Almost there, my muscles twitch from
the Tourette syndrome of my testosterone.
Damn, wasn't able to release her ocean.
Soaked in sweat stained sheets lay to strangers
married since forever.
[i]'m left frustrated, falling short of my man tower.

[i] need something
to keep the pontificating demons out of my head,
to turn off the tape recorder of the day,
to help me become submerged with sleep,
to mark a notch in the belt of Time.

When [i]'m finished,
[i] roll like a disappointed dog onto my back
and wait to be touched by the Waterwalker.
That's the only climax that will get me off.
That's the only orgasm that will
purge the virus of my soul's hardrive.
Until then, [i]'ll continue to
jack-off dry seeds of lost hope.

The Mirror

The mirror is not an exercise in perception.
It is a stenograph of Plato's Truth.
[i] may interpret and skew,
but the document never changes.
My hate for the mirror is mostly reflective energy.

My Thanksgiving stomach, my round Christmas cheeks,
my wide-load rear, in the pit of my esteem,
ugly is a cuckoo clock stuck on twelve.

The mirror is not an op-ed column,
but its voice is a morning alarm that [i] can't reach
from the sunken hole in my bed.
The mirror is a Truth that kicks more ass than sets me free.

The mirror knows no words smothered
with the sweet icing of subjectivity,
but its scientific lens shows the sloth in my soul.
It does no critical, supplemental reading,
but its juxtaposition of sizes creates titanic meaning.

Look closer, deep into the concave soul of the glass.
It's smiling a transparent grin of the ages,
closer to Aristotle's poet than we think.

Lowell's Beethoven

How long remained the ivory, marble-linked chain
clasped around my throat?
[i] submitted myself to your surveys, and was given
the runt's share of milk, then passed over like spoiled peas.
[i] was an apple trying to grow in a pecan orchard.
Your sour scholastic system has no eyes for me.
Your grades strangle me like heavy air,
squeezing and pumping me for every drop of my esteem.
The leaves of your pale anthology are cold and withered.
With every read, they erode.
History is a reference book, not a blueprint.
[i] am not Othello. [i] am not Aaron.
And yet all of Lowell's recipes are anthologized,
gathered to be dissected by the scientists,
but never savored by the hungry.
Beethoven be never more!
All of our sentenced times will come, poets.
We, they will duplicate, transcribe, and calculate
the chemistry of our colors, separating Beauty from Art.
This will be our death.
And we will then be the vogue of the vague.
In deafness Beethoven remained a slave
to the music in the chambers of his heart,
not a computer to the numbers,
and caused the reincarnation in the dry soil of Lowell.
Yet, there can be no GPA for creativity,
only a scientific scale plotting mimicry.
And [i] can never be Ben Johnson.
[i]'m just a deaf sheep herder with a psalm.

Memory

The Coz on the *Tonight Show*

Monday nights were the colored viewing section,
Johnny's furlough was like Black night at the fair.
Huddled in my cotton pajamas, colors no longer bold and
knees peeking through patches, my brown face splashed
with the lenient glow of the television lights from NBC's
proud and prancing peacock.
The layered, dancing, rainbow satin curtain pulled itself
back, and my heart would triple beat in excitement
when [i] saw his Earth-toned face appear.
A smile, the erupting discovery of involuntary emotion,
expands across the horizon of my face
as my eyes dance to his motions;
[i] study his soul food testifying language,
tasting every chocolate word of his lyrical buffet.

His presence felt like a chair that had always been
in grandma's living room.
If [i] closed my eyes, his voice fit like familiar furniture
in the den of my mind, like an evening hummingbird's call
or the similar smell of Sunday turnips and candied yams.
He had my uncle's brown, oak nut skin,
the same Black, course wool hair that lay on my head.
His wide nose raised and flared with his emotions.
Like my aunt's nose, it had smelled a lot,
surveying every scent before speaking.
His face told a story of his inherited antiquity
of which [i] could be an heir.
His narrative rang with the vibrating echoes of
my father's parable. It was a family reunion.

Oddly now, [i] realize this is my overture to race.
Johnny could, with a flashy phrase, evoke bursts of
laughter from the general satire of man's day-to-day,
but with the darker host my laugher grew from the seed
of the recognition of my me-ness in his him-ness.

His seasoned monologue dripped with
the sauce of my family fables,

his characters were neighborhood residents
who sat sheltered on my segregated street.
[i] could find his icons and punch lines
on the mustard coffee table in my house,
firmly planted between the private leaves of
Ebony pages and *Jet*-set style.
More than the Black guy on TV,
it was my patrimony in the flesh.
[i] existed, and the world knew it.
He was my trumpeter, my bard.
[i] vibrated with volcanic spasms of happy.
My life now extended pass
my gravel road youth and cotton field future.

Often, after she would kiss me goodnight,
my mother's swift got-to-be-somewhere walk would pause.
Her stern, school teacher's face
would soften and open like a night flower.
Slowly, turning off the television,
before her onyx face would disappear into the darkness,
[i] would see a lighthouse smile of pride, full even in
acknowledging her glowing embarrassment of giddy.
Proud of her brother, her uncle, her father,
her culture's journal in a picturesque light.
He was our best-selling biographer.
This is how the Coz "stood up" for us
when he "sat in" for Johnny on Monday nights.

The Smell of You on My Pillow

Why don't you catwalk 'round my crib anymore?
[i] miss seeing my floor decorated with your underwear.
My phone doesn't sing from the ring of your calls.
Yet even though you've taken away your body,
[i] can still smell your soul's scent in my hall.

There is an ache in my whole house for you.
My remote misses the touch of your hand.
My couch misses the dip and swerve of your curve
and the manner in which you make yourself
a mattress beneath your man.
My vanilla candles could never smell as sweet.
[i]'m tripping on the table in the kitchen
because you are more filling than vegetables.

My one bedroom crib is like an empty castle.
It makes room for the echo of my heart.
Like the echo of hollow pain pounding on my window,
[i]'m living off the smell of you on my pillow.

Does his tongue flick and slither against you
like the autumn air ringing the wind chimes
of your porch's soul?
Is his hallway just for walking?
Has he discovered
what a well angled shower head can do for you?
Is his living room just for talking, or have you turned it
into a den of Dionysius' wildest daydreams?

Don't you miss how [i] played your body like a piano?
We made secretly screaming sounds in space
not yet explored by Monk.
Every inch, crack, and crevasse of this house,
are just visions of positions that my video game can't take.

My one bedroom crib swells
like a river flooding with tears,
and there is not enough sunshine

to make the pain disappear.
The aroma of our love is a rising and crashing billow.
[i]'m a drowning clown
living off the smell of you on my pillow.

When only the stars are awake,
[i] bury my face in the space of your smell.
My body still fits the grooves and the indention
of the frame you left etched in the bed.
Like a manic monkey [i] grind away all my memories,
of things that we used to do,
intoxicated by the residue
of the lingering pheromone in my head.

My one bedroom crib is the Astrodome,
and [i] stand ready on the mound with no batter at home.
And like a country boy who can smell
the rain coming over the levee's meadow,
[i]'m living off the smell of you on my pillow.

> "Rock me baby, rock me all nite long…
> roll me baby, like my back ain't got no bone"
>
> B. B. King

Pecola's Dance

[i] met this hazy, blue-eyed, midnight girl,
exiled to the damp cerebral corners to her shoebox world.
Like a lonely hooker finding a wet puppy,
she took me home.
Her eyes, like my hair, come in a can.
Two half-priced damaged goods spending some time
licking their wounds.
She took me to her padded room,
turned the music up loud,
so it would flood and fill the cracks,
not letting other voices seep into our chipped groove.
Said this now was a bag of weed better than the crowd.
In her room with a cracked window view,
we bathed and were baptized by
insanity and the moonlight.
For a few moments pain lived somewhere else,
we making only the sounds of belonging…
all night long,
to her favorite blues song.

Daydreaming of a Wife on the Pascagoula Beach

[i] was lying entangled with my thorny emotions
in a brick bed of loneliness when within sealed eyes
a tiny bead of canary light began to blossom against an
infinite sea of charcoal night. As the light began to
mushroom, it took shape and walked toward me.
Her name was female and so was her body.
She introduced herself as Evening,
and asked if [i] knew the Dawn.
[i] replied, "No, but I am on my way to meet Her."
We laughed silent cries which ricocheted through my soul
while we discussed Nature, peaches, baked chicken, and
pecan pie. God is food, you know?
Noticing my opened shirt, she asked if she could
feel my heart to see if it was concrete.
In that moment of her silk touch of righteous restoration,
[i] could feel it expanding the longer she stayed,
the longer [i] gazed at the sway of her healthy hips.
[i] wanted to be baptized in her ocean lips and heaven eyes,
becoming lost in a thunderous sea of electricity.
Just the type of sista who would let you be
reborn through her ancient waterfalls.
So, as the specked white and Black birds flew o'er head
the bountiful, blushing breeze blew upon our bodies
cutting through me…([i] become
a leaf enduring a Spring shower.)
with every brush of the wind's hands upon my body.
Then she smiled as if she wanted to be us
the whole time…and we made a tribute to Eve's garden.

Just the trinity of us: her, [i], and Nature,
on a breezy beach day when wind kisses
remove the dirt of our history,
the water washing at the point
where all of our edges converge,
and we dissolve like life's powder into
something greater than the now that we know.
Mississippi sand sifts like brown sugar
on soft skin as the dusk sky became a canvass

finger-painted by magnolias angels.
Then she stood over me, sand dripping from her figure,
leaned like a willow tree and kissed my cheek.
The bright light that was her
disappeared into the space behind my eyelids,
and the Easter blue space turned a swirling, sunset
orange, then blurring into a pearl, onyx space.
[i] was baptized on a Pascagoula Beach,
filled with the Holy Ghost of Nature
where my wife and [i] became one seed.

Birdland's Angels

[i] need to vomit tears from the pit of my pain,
but [i] have lain in capitalism's thorny arms too long.
My rusted-iron soul can only clang an erratic, spastic tune.
It's a civil war of frustration.
With no pressure valve, [i] stand a contorted pretzel
on the edge of sanity's shimmering shores.
But, in a corner on a shabby stool, in a hole in the wall,
[i] can sit alone, close my windows, and listen to Time.
Within a few measures, they melt my metal interior.
[i] can hear Nature's song;
the wind and rain echo in four-four time.
My heart beats with their snapping syncopation.
Horns moan for me; horns moan for me.
Tears, sweet, gentle, baptizing tears,
cascade like a falling note down my cheeks.
[i] remember how to cry. It's my soul's orgasm
brought on by their tranquilizing noise,
releasing the pressures of my soul's stone dam,
playing my fears and doubts in a melody.
They lay healing hands on me, and my eyes can rain.

[i] need to ejaculate jovial jazz from my throat,
but insecurity's cold fingers make a mute of me.
Too afraid to laugh, too alone to laugh,
[i] hear a half note.
It dances and skips up the scales.
Playfully, it hides and seeks, peeks and boos.
Watching that half note in my mind
is like seeing a back-yard squirrel frolic from tree to tree,
and [i] find the laughter that was hidden
in the junky pocket of my heart.
It's like rekindling an old love on a winter's eve.
It comes to me like a tidal wave.
[i] remember running barefoot after a Delta shower,
through the grainy streets and slick alley ways,
treading like a homeward heading solider through
muddy cotton and soybean fields.
[i] ran weightless, a leaf floating on the wind of Time

just like that little smiling half note.

The sounds of the musicians are just their souls responding.
It's a pulpit and an amen corner
with each one driving the car along peace's parkway,
sometimes a preacher,
serenading us with a sermon,
sometimes a deacon,
yes-sir-ing and amen-ing the other along,
always conveying the blue-transient lives of us all.
They are the weighted voices of Time's pain
communing at the speak-easy church of Birdland.
You can call them Tri-tone.
My soul's ear calls them angels.

A Girl Named Chris: A College Classmate

[i] knew a girl named Chris;
she often sat on the couch of my mind.
She liked the taste of similar soaked cherries.
She was a samesexual lover searching
for Truth in a world full of cloudy mirrors.
The hole in her heart made finding love
like trying to catch rain with your hands
or walking through the snow in soleless shoes.
That's why her love was so raw.
We used to make funny faces all through the night.
She said my sex was a watermark above alright,
but it didn't satisfy her feline appetite.
She got straight A's and was a dancing girl.
She had the finest body and fished for the finest girls.
A Forlorned fawn, Chris spent so many nights sequestered
in the plastic prison of arbitrary reality—sentenced to
the maximum security lockdown of normality.
Instead of being clutched by a man,
she wanted to be sanctified in a woman's arms.

[i] knew a girl name Chris.
We used to talk under secret covers on the phone.
She'd cry all night from needing a woman's warm charm.
A bi and a try finding comfort in each other's arms.
Some nights we didn't surrender to sleep
'til the resurrection of dawn.
She just wanted to be held
by somebody who'd swam her waters.
[i] knew [i] wasn't Prince's Bambi,
but [i] did the best [i] could.

[i] knew a girl name Chris
who soon disappeared like evaporated rain
with only the wind to whisper her goodbye.
But her leaving was as predictable as the changing seasons.
The pillows of my heart remain perpetually soaked
from the thick tears of her soul.
[i] always think about her when the mist smothers days.

Still when the rain reluctantly falls,
[i] can hear her name in the light sidewalk patter.
She'd lie on top of me
and let her pounding organ beat upon my chest
for she really wanted a lover who could share her space
with interchangeable parts that she could undress.
[i] hope that she's got love and nothing less.

[i] knew a girl named Chris.
She was my favorite friend.
[i] hope she found tootsie rolls and lollipops in the end.

Anxiety

A Poet not by Choice

I

It feels like someone is fornicating or defecating
in my ear hole, leaving their release on my brain
that spawns into mold, which eventually
crumbles out of my mouth.

II

Eyelids reversed down to the locked position,
it's the closed-for-business sign being hung for the night.
Inside, the projector continues to play;
single words encoded with more than naming,
morphemes continuing to cascade and bombard.
Externally, my tinted eye-covers twitch and shudder
from the exploding impact of yellow electrons.
Words, electronic sperm, come together and form
waves of semantics and converge as lakes to a river,
the point which spurs the sleeping body to
dance involuntarily beneath the covers.
This is a lottery no one wants to win.

III

Read words linger after the final falling action.
Images of the color wheel pop in and out as muted
meanings slowly fade into the next vision.
My mind is aroused.
The pen allows for an orgasm,
bringing short showers of relief
until the next erection of a brain throbbing with ideas.
This is not pleasure, but a constant longing to jack-off.
Most nights a writer masturbates his pains away,
words either exploding in a fit of chaos
or oozing from a lumped flow of ideas.
But slaves never choose the moment of work.

IV

Most volunteer, the Artist is captured—
a wild animal that society wishes to domesticate
only to be "put down" for biting the hands that imprison it.
The Artist is drafted like Saul or kidnapped like Jonah.
Though some choose to make their vessel
capable to carry the cargo, the intuitive act of organizing
words is more akin to a mother bird building its first nest.
Creativity may be honed, but the pregnancy is immaculate.
And if allowed to grow, my mind barely remains mine.
It's the wait station for words which appear,
biding time for their next destination.
The mind is merely a port, not a nation,
filled with transient ideas longing to find havens
in the community of language.
And this need to play social worker
to a bunch of orphaned and homeless morphs
is a desire born in heaven's well of words,
edited by pontificating angels,
channeled through the workshop of your mind,
and controlled by the Garden's Architect.
It's not your choice to make.
Death is the only retirement for the Artist.

To You

For the horizon of the weekend,
the only budding flowers of my mind have been you.
That last day on the floor, us together,
intertwined and locked like vines,
pressed tightly together like kneaded dough.
It's a film playing in my mind.
[i] am still shadowed by your Black dress with soft
yellow and swirling raspberry pink flower prints,
your feather frame lying upon mine.
That shining sloping curve in your lower back
which seductively slinks and swings into the curl
of your melon-rounded, pearl of an ass.
You are a vision of plum and passion, the lingering smell
and taste of your caramelized ambrosia keeps me coming
back like orphaned water returning to the receiving sea.
My dumb ass is in love with you.
[i] feel like the freshman pig-tailed school girl
fallen heels over head for the senior ballplayer.
My manhood doesn't like that.
My petrified, pouting penis reminds me of my ego,
but my heart's melted magnet spins me to you.
[i] am a bird flying south for the warmth of you.
[i] ache for the juju healing power of you.
[i] can't stop needing to hear your cotton soft calming
voice fall upon my ear in the still of a Mississippi night.
All at once [i] am man and mouse.
In the heat of our moments, [i] am Shaka,
but in a flip of a phrase [i] become your board game.
You have inverted the stone statues of our roles;
Virginia Woolf and Alice Walker would be proud.
My amputated maleness wants to be forever blind to you.
Yet with one slide of your finger,
my manhood stands at attention.
Your blanket of grace amazing,
your sharp and biting fury castrating.
Parts of me are grateful for having been your fool.
But now [i] ask that you emancipate me
from the captivity of Miss Cellie's curse.

Don't say my name anymore, not with that mouth;
that mouth could make rain defy gravity.
To hear my name liquefied breathlessly across your
lips is to be crucified every time you speak.
[i]'m drunk with you (way past twelve steps).
Life with you is a constant swirl of heaven and hell,
converging endlessly on themselves.
How quickly tears of joy are turned into streaks of sorrow.
Explosions of laughter fizzle into a residue of pain,
and yet, the more of myself [i] lose
is worth the memories [i] gain.
Confusion is the child of our fling.
You are a prism of a rainbow of emotions.
Never am [i] one color for very long.
[i] am continuously dissolving
from twig weak to oak wood strong.
You wear a smiled frown embedded on your blank face
from having drowned me in your Venus Flytrap,
leaving me with emotions that reek as waste.
A pocket full of soiled memories is what [i] have.
Be gone "O" meat eating, bloody fanged Beauty.
Take thy disguised dagger from my heart and let me die.
The fumes of the memories will dull the pain…

[i] Hate Christmas

Christmas is a sick, deranged monster
with rusty ass claws and crocked, dull fangs,
the kind that puncture the skin and soul,
leaving a chewed hole in my essence.
He enjoys coming around every twelve months
just to poke a hole in my cracker-thin security.
Christmas is the deformed Igor of man's misplaced
intentions, capitalism's crippled cousin whom we keep
closed in the closet until the apex of my year,
causing a trembling of my loose inners that reaches
far into the crowded basement of my psyche.
Here he comes again, just on the heels of
Kill an Njun and Take His Land Day.
We sell souls in this country.
He creeps in with the first real crisp wind of the year,
seducing us all with deluded memories
of childhood bliss and toys that frame our innocence.
Before you know it, this virus is spreading
throughout the neighborhood—
a green and red bow mysteriously placed on a door;
then a couple of days later,
some single, isolated fool is on his rooftop,
orchestrating multicolored lights
around the edges of his home
so that none of us will be able to sleep.
Then, passing by someone's window,
there it is, the true symbol of this
mockery of mankind's intelligence,
the Evergreen, decorated like an ugly ass drag queen.
Yet, it's not Christmas time 'til that single call is heard,
Nat "King" Cole's liquid, seductive voice
ushering in a full season.
From his grave he's laughing at us.
In my weakened state, [i] crumble like last year's fruitcake.
How the fuck am [i] going to be able to afford
the total cost of Yule Tide Gladdenings?
Each year December twenty-fifth is staring at me
from June fifteenth.

It's smiling at me and my rag doll self.
LAY-AWAY is the only way of the poor,
too under-approved to finance
too over-approved for the Salvation Army.
Stuck in the lagoon's middle of Christmas and Damnation,
my step-children waiting on a reason to demand divorce.
And for this gumbo of emotions, [i] hate Christmas.
Where is Baby Jesus when you need Him?
[i] think [i]'ll convert to being a Jehovah's Witness
'til just after January two.
Then [i]'m pardoned from the seasonal lie of liking y'all.
For it is Christmas when [i] am drowned
under the shade of mortality,
a helpless and hopeless flower suffocated by a larger tree.
When without a word, God fills the pockets of my soul.
Every twelve months, [i] become
a motherless child again, and [i] detest the dried taste
of defenselessness on my tongue.
Every twelve months, the enormous
gift-giving avalanche emasculates me, and my insecurity
sprouts like bathroom mold.
God, without a word, fills the pockets of my pants.
And [i], in my empty book of knowledge, resent it.
Christmas is too complex for my nervous system.
God becomes a puzzle with pieces
[i] own but have misplaced.
[i] am extended into space by a hand that's
connected to nothing. The grip is firm and warm,
but there is nobody to which it is anchored.
And this dichotomy dissects me.
That's why [i] hate Christmas.

To the Musician

There's a bouncing voice inside me
that's raging flame to come out.
It strikes and stabs at my soul, leaving me bleeding,
slowly suffocating from the inside. My whole body aches,
for [i] wasn't given your gift to churn the milk of emotion
into the butter of sound like flowers turn poison into breath.
My body has no unclogged aperture
for this creature to escape.
It's like a fire in my building,
and [i]'m tripping off the smoke.
[i] try to speak, but my gravel tonsils
slice the sounds trying to defect.
[i]'m a musical mute, a bucket full of holes
than can't hold a note.
> [i] would gladly go to the cross tomorrow
> for just one moment of release,
> just to spew the seed sounds of my soul.
> Then [i] could expire in peace.

Chaos is the sound of my thoughts.
Disorder my holy ghost.
My body is a temple in ruins,
withered from spoiled, aborted harmonies.
The sounds inside me are stuck on a raft without a sail,
never finding the land of expression because
[i]'m unable to navigate the calculus of a musical scale.
[i]'m heavy and constipated from a raw meat rhythm.
There is much internal bleeding.
My sandpaper vocal chords weren't built for harmonizing.
My musical mind is dyslexic;
it can't read the groove in my head. [i] long to vomit the
leftover notes from the sharpened songs trapped in my
mind, which cut, slice, and poke holes in my brain.
> Music is a slippery salamander slicing
> through the fingers of my mind;
> Just to hold one note in the palm of my
> throat would shatter the pain and stop time.

> "You got to go full tilt bozo. You were only
> given a little spark of madness so don't ever
> lose it…because it keeps you alive."
> Robin Williams

Hold on to Your Insanity

The well-dressed carnival clowns
have waged war on the insane.
It's open season on the mentally disturbed,
as if it's our fault that our brains are too big for our bodies,
or is it that our creativity overcrowds the closets
of our minds, or is it that our imagination
is a river that floods their dry reality?
Don't let 'em take your insanity away from you.
Being sick is simply a liberation from
the castrated normality that surely leads
to a mid-life dive into the pool's deep end.
It's the peculiar people; we are the children of the Sun.
And we didn't even ask to be planted in this scorched soil.
Tomorrow equates to a bucket of waste to us.
Hell, all of my todays and yesterdays look like twins.
So, erase from your mind the mathematicians
who looked in the back of the book for the answer;
it still doesn't mean that they can solve for X and Y,
which are slipping on the slop of sliding sanity like a church
girl who doesn't know how she got dirty panties.

Fantasy is the acting agent of reality…
Your words build a nest in my heart, George.

They, the normal mockingbirds trying to assimilate me.
Nietzsche!?! Are the waters muddy enough for you?
Yet, yo' ass went crazy, didn't you.
Swimming in shallow waters will do that to you.
You stayed up there too long, man!
You stayed away too long, man!
Why would you want them malignant mockingbirds
to understand you anyway?
What made you think that people with concrete vision could
understand a man with water-flowing dreams?
Don't worry because Heidegger and Derrida

molded and mainstreamed yo' jazz
like Texas Instruments modified the scientific calculator
for any fool looking for the square root of zero.

My mind is mine no matter how muddy it is.
[i] didn't fill out no application to be here.

They, the contracted scholars,
trying to put my round peg into their square ideology.
They tell me to, "Cut my hair!"
[i] tell them to, "Grow some integrity!"

Damn you and the Theory of Consolidation, Downsizing, and
Mainstreaming 404 course you took
to improve your Dow Jones value with the world.
You and your Borg mentality,
if resistance is futile, then [i]'ll drink a cup of death.

"Jesus, save me with your red wine!"

My God, why have thou left me on this rugged cross?
Janie, baby, [i] need you;
they want my inside Janie.
[i] need your pear tree.
Can you save one more Teacake?

The insane are scared. The sane are paranoid,
locked in this windowless room together.
None of us want to sleep.
My soul weighs like a falling anvil.
It's dark; [i] can hear the sistas on the mother board.

"[i]~~~~[i] love the Lord; He heard my cry."

Why am [i] holdin' on…
why am [i] holdin'…
why am [i]…
why am…
why…

[i] need sleep with my dreams…

The Unrequited Calling
(For Jonah, Moses, Medgar, and Martin)

Jesus is chasing me.
Like a centipede, he's crawled up my back.
He digs his fingers into my spine.
[i]'m a plastic flower planted in concrete.
He's Jim Henson looking for another puppet.
His heavy hot tongue flicks and flashes against my ear.
His penetrating virile voice echoes loudly inside me.
It continues to bounce off my hollow insides.
It is searching for fertile soil inside my barren soul.
There's nobody home.

"Stop it!" [i] scream from the intestines of my soul.
Jesus smiles at me from the cross.
[i] find myself kneeling before this cheap Easter ad.
His crimson chrism drips ferociously upon me,
burning whelps and holes into the skin of my resistance.

Jesus is chasing me; He wants a spokesman…
no He wants my borrowed soul.
[i] won't give it to Him; He'll kill me for it.
(Jesus is medieval.)
[i] don't want to expire. My soul is nauseous.
My flesh crawls with creeping consternation.
Jesus wants me; all governments need expendable soldiers.

"Leave me alone!" rings from my ego.
He mocks my flaming ignorance with His smothering love.
He makes me feel the thorns against His head.
He smiles and waits.

Jesus is chasing me; my mouth is dry.
My throat feels of hot razors
sucking for evaporating air and water.
My belly burns of the hot coals,
which is the seething starvation of lacking scripture.
It growls and grumbles, vibrating throughout me.
My head palpitates viciously from hunger.

My sweaty, swollen feet burn of one million miles
aching to the bone, twitching and throbbing
with every step.

"Go Away!" the roots of my phallus demands.
Even though [i] run from Him,
he prepares a table for my misdirected journey.
[i] stop. [i] sit. [i] rest. [i] eat.
My belly is full of the fruits of His juicy Charity.
He mocks me with His Covenant.

Like prey whose predator is gaining on him,
every ounce of my being is used to elude Him.
My quick-sanding steps multiply.
[i] glance back through the dust of my speed and realize,
damn, He's gaining on me.
His hand is on my shoulder.
One hand is on both shoulders?
He won't let go. It's a long run from Jesus.
[i] give Him the slip, down the alley,
around the corner liquor store and into
a house of ill repute.
He'll never find me here.

A skinny Black girl with hair of wool gazes into my eyes. She takes me home, and we wash each other's feet. We break wheat bread together. There is more fish than [i] could ever eat. Time undresses who [i] was. She takes my name, gives me her womb, and saves my soul.

Love(?)

The Beat of my Love

Understand that your ears are more valuable than your mouth.
So, don't make any noise that may drown our salvation.
Lie perfectly still and listen with your soul as
the beat of my love calls to you, begs to you, longs for you
like a starving baby longing for his mother's breast milk.
It's an untamed horse, thumping and jumping for you.
Each beat is a second counting down
the volcano that erupts for you.
Like the sounds of a dark jungle,
big cats roar and purr, and trees sing and sway with wind.
Tribal drums play along the moonlight,
and the Earth rotates to its rhythm.
You are the drummer; you control the beat,
playing my heart like a snare.
Is that a high hat [i] hear?
Does it pound against your anima?
Straddle this beat and ride.
The rhythm is Eros. Syncopation is my style.
Wild emotions run river free. The beat swells and grows,
running from you back to me,
bouncing like bumble bees atop nature's wet breeze.
The Narrator in heat; He must feel the beat.
We could dance a while, Relax your groove and stay.

Do we tell the rain to stop from falling?
Do we tell the waters to stop from flowing?
Do we tell the Sun to stop from shining?
As with tides to the Moon, as with children to recess,
as with planet population to sex,
just like gravity will never cease,
just like the rivers rushing to the sea,
as long as little boys pull freshly plaited pigtails,
drums will keep time, and we will move,
continuing to swim up stream navigated
by the internal throbbing to forge ahead;
this is the beat…the beat of my love.

You Are Sex

From the first moment you walked through
the entrance doors of my vacant life,
you have been a flick that plays in my mind.
You are constantly on rewind.
You have a website on my brain.
Scenes and fantasies of you are
saved, filed, and bookmarked.
You are to the orgasm what
sun and rain are to vegetation—
You, alone, are an orgasmic trinity.

You are sex:
Your body is a map on the roadway to eruption.
Your coffee toned skin, one milk three sugars,
smooth as wet spring flowers
and sweet as powdered cinnamon.
Your thighs fill a room like well-defined furniture
as your legs seem to cascade like
piping hot fudge melting chocolate ice cream.
The natural smell of you drives me wild,
smelling like butterscotch orgasm laced with
sun sweetened peaches.
Your passion is a running faucet,
dripping all over your inner thighs.
You are too much to spoon. [i] need a cup.
You want me…to drink…myself full of you.
And once drunk with you,
my firm honesty slowly slides against your
soaked walls of truth.
They expand and contract like a python against me,
milking me of my juices.
Exploration feels good, going into
the deeper recesses of your uncharted globe.

You are sexuality:
You soul is a plush, inner comfort sanctuary that
keeps you free from the currency of guilt and shame
that has paralyzed the rest of us.

Every release is a baptism, cleansing the soul
of lost Adams and oppressed Eves.
Your knowledge of yourself liberates your rivers.
You refuse to subscribe to prescribed notions of
Chastity and Spinster-hood.
You're a liberated slave who has
wrested freedom from your masters.
You want it done so well that
your soul shakes for seven days.
For you, being wet is part of being human.
It's this attitude that causes you
to colonize my ass with you eyes.
You wonder if [i] will understand
your need to be on top.
You want a man who is not a slave to normality,
who will pump you full of bulging masculinity,
and still understand your need for flowers of femininity.
Your sexual tree is rooted in the soil of freedom.
The orgasm is the alpha and the omega.
(Let's be Frank 'cause if we can't be Frank
who can we be?)
Having your body explode is the
central issue of your book.

You are fantasy:
You are the wet dream
of every unsatisfied person on this planet.
The actress in you has played every possible role
of what we want but are afraid to claim.
For you have the universal keys that unlock the door
or the knife that cuts the ropes separating desire and reality.
For most people, the wall of fear
stands between their fantasy and reality.
Fantasy, for you, is only that meal which
you have not had the opportunity to eat.
When opportunity opens, like a Pullman Porter,
you usher fantasy across the threshold into reality.
This is when you become the trinity to which
[i] gladly offer my body up to that cross.

[i] wonder can you talk to your man?
Can you trust his cup of manhood
to hold all of your liquid fantasies?
Or, do you suffer from sexual diarrhea,
leaving a trail of your overflow where you go?
Can he handle you needing to open the valves
to your streams just to make it through another day?
[i] don't know if [i] can; but [i]'d gladly drown
in the waves of your crashing oceans, sacrificing myself
for the fulfillment of your Black widow desires.

The Reading of the Kiss

How many kisses does it take to get to know you?
How many times 'til [i] recognize every kiss
and know what each one means?
When will [i] be able to read
the slight subtleties and nuances of the touches of your lips
and know the difference from kiss to kiss?

With the brush of your lips, [i] hear you say,
"You can stay."
With the slide of your tongue, [i] hear you say,
"I surrender."
With the moan of your throat, [i] hear you say,
"Good Gawd, don't stop."
With a purposeful press of your lips, [i] hear you say,
"Find the backroom of my pleasure."

How long does it take to feel the heat from your mouth
and know how you want your fires stoked?
When will [i] feel the touch of your tongue against mine
and know that you wish for me to explore further?
[i] can't wait for the moment [i] know that you want
a peck to undress into a kiss and disrobe into more.

Morris-coded into every kiss
are the messages drummed by lovers.
So when will [i] know that one kiss which signals that
this kiss is as unique as April snow in a Mississippi spring?
'Cause when in translation between lovers,
not one thought can be hit or miss,
especially when the deepest, darkest thoughts
of the heart are articulated with a kiss.

[i] want to know that the tears you cry
come from the gentle press of our lips,
and that when my tongue enters inside
your heart explodes like ten thousand landmines.
Then [i]'ll know the secrets of how to kiss you,
and the one kiss you need to erase the color blue.

[i] want to hear every thought of every kiss
and know exactly what it is that you want me to do.
[i] want to know that the moisture of your lips
is calling me to take a dip into the sea of your soul.
And when [i] press, you press back,
[i]'ll know that you want me to pull
all of the colors out of Black.

When your lips linger, [i] hear
"This is where [i] want to be."
When your tongue flicks, [i] hear
the dam breaking beneath your levee.
When your mouth sucks my air, [i] hear
"How close do we have to get to become one?"
When your lips mold themselves to mine, [i] hear
the combination to your heart click and open…

Everyday Is another Day to Fall in Love with You
(A Poem for my Wife)

Everyday is another day to fall in love with you.
But everyday that [i]'m with you,
[i] can't believe that it's true 'cause you are
the warm inside of summer that lasts long into the winter;
you are a brown, cinnamon strawberry licorice
that brings syrupy euphoria with every kiss.
And when [i]'m not with you,
it's the smell of your soul that [i] miss.
Everyday with you is like the excitement of the first moon;
it's a fourth of July explosion on a Christmas afternoon.

Everyday is another day to fall in love with you.
And every night that brings the moon
is another holiday gone too soon.
[i] like to wallow in your oceans,
each river breaking a dam.
Your love is a cool spring running
where my soul may take a dip.
And if you pour you heart into a glass and offer it up,
[i] can't help but take a sip.
The finest nectar, you have matured with time;
and everyday with you is glorioso fine.

Everyday is another day to fall in love with you.
For you continue to be an open window to my view.
And every night that [i]'m baptized within you
brings another morning resurrecting me anew.
You are my female reflection.
We are of one soul sculpted from two.
You are my Sun-rising salvation whose rays [i] use to
wade through any fog-covered swamp to get back to you.
Connection has made us a butterfly,
and to feel your heart pound against mine
is laughter deeply embedded inside a cry.
Now [i] no longer know the color blue
for everyday is another day to fall in love with you.

Concerns

Where Is the Temple of My Familiar?

[i] saw the temple of my familiar years before Judas' kiss,
faintly remembering the legacy of my yester being,
my organic origin from the pits of the universe.
But somewhere,
along the journey of someone else's story,
my circle has been broken.
[i] no longer know how to posses the secrets of joy.
My skin is scratched by somebody else's clothes.
Like a receding hair line, [i] move, am removed,
from the dirt of my DNA, becoming just another
copy of a copy of a copy of my lost Ideal.
Yet my mind remains haunted by
the flaky remnants of the Truth of my loss.

And you wonder why [i]'m a rolling stone.
There can be no peace in a defiled temple
where lies fornicate with history.
My soul is an irate quadriplegic
trapped in the ruins of progress.
It's a tainted union that bears rotten fruit,
a civil war that destroys me like a worm
at an apple's core.
One thousand lives [i], myself, have lived
and still don't know the paragon of what is.
So, [i] kneel West and pray to Plato's Ideal.
Yet, my mind wonders, heeding the aroma
of Aristotle's subjectively soaked reality.
[i] can't find Home on somebody else's map.
Where the fuck is Africa when you need her?
All of these crippled and poisoned theories
create acid reflux in my soul,
as [i] hold on to Achebe's center to stay afloat.
Yet, the plotted planes of Brathwaite and Baraka
leave me alone on a re-centered atlas.

Death is only an opportunity to realize who [i] am,
for Time only measures the imprint of my footsteps.
Like Toomer, can [i] be so certain and so wrong?

Or, will Time show him at the center
and the rest of us at the edges, clinging to our limitations?
As the faces and theories jingle in my mind
like a broken jig-saw puzzle,
none of their pants fit my rounded rear end.
My memory is jailed
by its cemented connection to the physical;
it now suffers from Alzheimer's,
for my mind is no longer mine.

Where is the temple of my familiar?
Where is my familiar temple?
If our eyes are watching God, what do we see?
How can we be so close and not see forest or tree?

One thousand generations locked away by undeciphered
hieroglyphics left on the abandoned and ruined walls.
[i] need Brother Ray to show me the One
when it's buried beneath the twang of another's story.
My soul hears, but my mind can't grasp the call.
Has it withered like an unread anthology?
Or, is it just misplaced because [i]
don't know my authentic nature.
Tomorrow's years will bring one thousand more lives.
Will they have to find one thousand more realities?
When [i] arrive back to my Penelope, will [i] know where
my temple is, and will [i] have mind to recognize it?

To Be Post-Colonial Isn't to Be Re-indigenous (?)

Who draws a line in the murky sand of life and says,
"Things change here"?
Does a colonizer's sword shred antiquity in two
like Swiss cheese.
Can a colonized man regain his indigenous wrapping?
Does he want to?
Is post-colonial a gumbo of pieces forever melted.

>You can never go home again,
>said the man whose house was stolen
>by Time's blind accessories.

The visiting college student, home on the weekend,
always realizes the smallness of the kitchen.
With which eye does the colonized African
see the shifting land under his new shoes?
With which eyes does the New and Improved African
see his fading footsteps from home?
Do we wanna go home?

>Is post-colonial a jacket [i] can wear?

Does it mean that the visiting, squatting foreigner
is no longer kicking your ass from your own living room,
but he's still kicking your ass from his plush porch
by remote control across the sea?
Or, is being post-colonial
removing the Frankenstein iron clamps from your brain and
the stigma of servitude from your brain's filmy eyes
so that you can see yourself...anew?
Does the new creature want to live in the old home?
Is post-colonial a rebirth
of the sovereignty of culture of the indigenous?

Can a man go back into the womb?

Where is my terra firma? Where is my tongue?
Will [i] find it if [i] return to before,

or will [i] find Africans disassociated from Alkebu-lan?
Can we see Kemet with our blue eyes?
Where is my welcome mat?
[i] wanna feel the organic flow of energy between my
cushioned toes as [i] stand barefoot on cool stability.

Where's my head-rest?
How do you get to there from here
when here equates to the destruction of there?
Are we standing on the verge of being on the verge…?
[i] know how to get to Sesame Street;
can you tell me how to get to Indigenous Land?

In a secret room down the stairway of our minds,
our inners remember paradise.
It tugs like a restless child at our comatose consciousness,
affirming that everything is not on cement foundation.
Can we return from Adam's slip?
Can we reconvene our meeting with the universe?
Or, is it an urban renewal project where we, new creatures,
return to homes inhabited by strangers?
And, how do we know that we are not the strangers?

> "His attitude with black
> [southerners] is yet more frightening,
> for he appears to despise them for
> never having braved the North.
> They, on the other hand, counter that
> they have friends and relatives in the
> North, and, on the other hand, appear
> to despise him because he lacked the
> courage to remain in the South."
> from *Just Above my Head*
>
> James Baldwin

Letter to the Northern Negro

We gave you roots, and with your ax of iron living
you chopped them off.
We gave you the underground railroad.
You gave us the Colombian Connection.
We gave you Negro spirituals.
You took the snowman's philosophy and
reasoned God from the sky.
We told you to "Cast down your buckets where you are."
You padded your palms with food stamps.
You're killing yourself with half-baked
bloody and borrowed intelligence,
hip to the ways of civilization's false, straw-hut progress,
hip to the ways of capitalism slick, double-sided tongue,
hip to the ways of mercantilism's purple pimpism,
hip to the ways of assimilation's suffocating fur coat,
hip to the ways of the caste system's stone shoes.

We planted a forest of Life; you bring us termites,
packed in frosted, cubed tobacco pellets
and co-opted commoditified liberation.

Take back your crystal seeds of white death.
Take back your Black Klans.
Take back your automatic iron arrows.

They may not come from the womb of your ingenuity, but
you remain a begging child gladly accepting your step-
father's machines of mass mail order destruction.

You've turned the South from tilling fields to killing fields.
The Southern Negro never ate his own, never paraded
his own for the perverse phallic pleasure of others.
Yet, we are imprisoned in a plantation mentality(?)
We used to run North to escape lynchings.
Now, you run South to escape your sorry soaked seeds.
We are forced to hide you in our cotton bosom
when you flee your unkempt metal beds.
Run-away urban slaves,
you are an evil virus that migrates here,
infecting us with your decaying shell of a spirit.

What our storehouse of "intelligence" lacks,
our sun sweet spirit supports,
as you have lost your potato pie pleasantness
to long frigid winters and the constant clang
of steel against steel.
You are a bronzed, industrialized soul
with the heart of the fanged oppressor,
and you take advantage of
your Southern brother's good will and desire
to be like his evolved, "liberated" brother.

Northern brother,
you are an epidemic inflicted upon us.
The only good that you've ever given us is Jazz,
and you carjacked that from New Orleans swing.

God Has a Napoleon Complex

God has a Napoleon Complex.
He is the audience to be pleased by this play.
That's why it's a shop project in His image.
He only wishes to fellowship
with good little carbon-copy servants.
And by being made in the image of the Creator,
we are all small, egotistical little tyrants.
Baby Napoleons is what we are.

Let's check it out.
What's the Brother's claim to fame?
He made the world.
So?
It ain't like we were filling out applications to be here.
And just look at the human being.
Now, that's some shoddy workmanship.
And you notice God ain't giving us
no guarantees on His work.
Oh yeah, there's a covenant here and there,
but nothing substantial on which
our soul can hang its hat.

God has a Napoleon Complex.
He ain't thinking 'bout no democracy.
He gives us our own will
so that He can punk us into being His concubines.
We give it all up for Him.
You can't fuck. You can't eat pig.
You can't scratch any of the itches that He created.
And, He'll pimp you against your own will.
Look at Paul,
one minute persecuting and the next preaching.
Talk about your Anti-Trust Law.
If that ain't a monopoly, what is?

If you don't think God has a Napoleon Complex,
stop paying them ten percent taxes He cloaks as tides.
See what happens to yo' ass then.

That's why you can't have no God before Him.
And you can keep your body.
That jalopy ain't worth much.
He wants that forever thing, your soul.
Now that's a long term contract.

God is a tyrant, and [i]'m a fool.
And by covenant,
He has to take care of me.

Tripping on my One

White vampires suck on feeble bones
as Black rag dolls choke on glass dependency.
Niggas and Honkeys can't even be food for trees.
Together, you don't equal to a whole anything.
You are all just the waste of history,
mindlessly moving, never evolving,
a clump of mass.
[i]'ll be so glad when society rolls over
so that individuals can take over.

In the plain,
sin is birthed from the sperm of society.
It's the offspring of man's relationship to man.
One plus God equals Love.
The extra mockingbird broke the connection.
The more the merrier?
Only if misery be thy name.
For it takes two people before
one of them can be vain.

Dress how they want you.
You are mass produced like your clothes,
buying your personalities and beliefs from the mall.
Don't wanna know anything that breaks the frozen ground.
Just wanna know what will keep you
firmly planted in the concrete of acceptance.
The only happenings in your world
are reactions to reactions.
And you call me pitiful as you
huddle in your safe masses
clinging to a shell of life
choking off the fumes of normality.
You would much rather be safe than sorry.
[i] would rather be free than safe.

Go ahead.
Chase me to the roof top,
placing me on the pedestal of otherness.

My mind is bankrupt of thoughts for you.
Your barracuda hostility towards me
only signifies that your lives
are soaked in gasoline fear.
Normality is the Big Rig that you drive
to run me off the narrow road of acceptance.
You put me in a windowless cage
so that my reflection
isn't a mirror showing you half-assed made.

Like an insecure lion eating orphaned cubs,
the nature of the society is to crush the individual
so that it can deteriorate in peace.

Have another doughnut you glutton.
[i] only hope that your heart attack comes soon
so that fresh flowers of freedom can bloom.

> "Now you can tear a building down,
> but you can't erase a memory.
> These houses may look all run down,
> but they have a value you can't see."
>
> Living Color, "Broken Memories," 1988

Open Letter to a College Professor

Just because you refuse to teach them, did you
really think they would evaporate like forgotten rain?
Don't you know that every branch has a root, and that
Nature makes every bird return to the place of the nest?
As a forest we still hear their echoes even though most
of our ears are filled with your chalky cotton lies.
But just be sure that as we stand
we will decipher Phyllis' distorted voice.

You tell us that we did not inscribe,
that slavery was our prelude into civilization.
Yet, the walls of the echoing Nile River tombs
are the preface to the entire world,
and still you've made us mute
when we've been double-tongued from the Genesis.
Yet, you treat brothers like Olaudah Equiano
like a weak limb in the tree of Western Expansion.

So many Black minds with your pasty PhDs
yet not one course in us you require.
Then you wonder why we're on fire.
A lifetime spent in study,
and not one semester spent on me.
Yet we continue to find a lush lexicon for our lives.

My mind is sentenced to six hours in Europe
with only a weekend pass to Africa.
You want me to be a bastard child to hide that
you are Dr. Weiss's thief that lurks in the night.
But you give me twenty-eight days to catch up

on the scribes whom you've shut up,
by deleting their names from the rolls of
Caucasian curriculums.

Our troubadours keep on appearing,
if not in suits, in t-shirts, blue jeans, and earrings.
The soul of a people will not be dammed
but will continue to flow washing away your myths.
Your abridged anthologies can't erase
the fact that we be here.
Like air and soil, we won't disappear
even if polluted by your evil.
We refuse to be eaten and swallowed by
the *Beowulf* of assimilation.

Without homes, a nation, or patrons,
we've managed to perpetuate our narratives,
signifying who is the real monkey,
restoring Eshu to the heavens.

Suicide Note

The Suicide Note

Dear Melted Masses:

If [i] didn't ask to be hatched, to whom do [i] owe any allegiance? Suicide, then, is not a cop out; it's an alternative to suffering. My contempt is for those who have lost sight of their true essence, the individual, and have clung like parasites to their degenerative, regressive state, the society. Yet if [i] didn't ask to be here, (and [i] didn't; that was some Saturday night choice made by my biological units when their brains were pumped full of happy juices.), then your rules can be flushed down my toilet to lie where they belong, in a soiled societal septic tank. Your socialization is merely a euphemism for brainwashing. And when [i]'m gone, you'll say "He couldn't handle it." or "He didn't have any faith." If the truth be known, the human species has turned my stomach with its sewage of hypocrisy since [i] could make the distinction that a "group" meant three people who are afraid to be alone. [i]'m not cowering from you; [i]'m just unable to hide my volcanic disdain for humanity any loner. Thus, suicide is my way of preventing my evolution to mass murderer.

We are a petrified forest. There are very few trees in our midst. We've become a retro-society of father knows best, allowing a blind father to lead us off the cliff as we mindlessly cast votes for the rhetoric of bullshit sandwiches that justifies our iniquities by blaming others for the smell of our own unwashed asses. Cracker-ass honkeys voting for cracker-ass honkeys; niggers voting for niggers. As the world turns in a wobbling and shaking manner, you myopic, civil rights people are still searching for a utopian tomorrow while all of our children are killing each other. Yet, you are too scared to open your eyes and face the edge of night. Well, fuck y'all very much, but your actions are not bold, and this world is not beautiful. But, lead on, the herd is following.

My brothers and sisters hanging out in the mall (The Great Temple of Normality) with their dreads, braids, and dashikis, all decked out in their red, black, and green, still giving their green to the monster of frosted capitalism as fuel for the machine to digest them, but, of course, [i]'m the sellout who ain't never been sold. [i] guess everybody needs a nigger, even niggas. My people talk about action, spend $125.00 on a pair of Nikes, and wonder what's wrong with our children. Yet, [i]'m crazy. (Can you name twenty Black authors? No? But, [i] bet yo' ass can name fifty professional athletes.) But we can march, can't we?

You cowards join organizations so you don't have to take responsibility for thinking for yourselves. Why am [i] never harassed by one person? [i] guess where two or more are gathered in the name of society, courage will arise. And Black people walk in a circular motion in the woods of no direction, waiting on another Negro Jesus to sacrifice his existence to show them the path that's already there. Read a fucking book, a magazine, a newspaper! My distain for the cowards gives me empathy for m-&-m killers, but my mind knows that only the Brother on the High Throne has the Right and Power to Judge. So, [i] take my leave so as not to overstep my bounds.

White paint has to work overtime to hide Black walls. Not to fight until death is to give in to slavery. White people flee the city; we run right behind them. Not even Negroes want to live in Black neighbors. You're weak as sugar water and pathetic as half pennies, praying to an intangible God, who, through you own ignorance and fear, is powerless and limp in your lives.

[i]'m not afraid of you, but [i] am ill with you. This suicide is my divorce from you. Too much of my life is connected to you. God planned it that way. My soul needs more. My mind needs more. [i]'ve had a headache since [i] was twelve. My soul has spasms from the thought of remaining plugged in to you. To hear the noise of your life is to sleep with a migraine. To say that [i] have lost faith is

to say that [i] once believe that this mountain of excrement could be molded like the potter's clay.

My soul has a hernia from the internal pain. [i] need some Rolaids from you, from this blurred copy of a copy. Life did come with a set of instructions. It's called the *Bible*, the *Koran*, the *Analects*, and the *Holy Book of Tao*. They've become impotent to me because of my inability to love you. For you don't believe in the divinity of the individual. Your true religion is normality, and we all fall short because none of us are normal. But, you can't see that because you've given yourself up to the cross of acceptance. Now you belong to them, and [i] only belong to me.

Eternally,
C. Liegh

Reconciliation

Am [i] a Hypocrite?

Am [i] a hypocrite because [i] wanna have sex
with every woman [i] meet, but [i] wanna marry a virgin?
Am [i] a hypocrite because
[i] wanna fall in love and marry,
but [i] wanna keep me a li'l sweet potato pie on the side?
Am [i] a hypocrite because [i] wanna purchase a family car
and still test drive the sleek sports cars,
but [i] wanna be my wife's only driver?
Am [i] a hypocrite because [i] have a li'l somphin'
somphin' on the side, but [i] want my woman to stay
planted by the phone, waiting on me to call for harvest?

Am [i] a hypocrite because [i] want to sail the night seas,
but [i] want my Penelope to stay home alone,
waiting on her Odysseus to return?
Am [i] a hypocrite because when [i] met you
[i] liked seeing you in those sexy clothes,
but now [i] want you in a potato sack from head to toe?

Am [i] a hypocrite, or am [i] a man?
And if [i] am a hypocrite, what does that make you
for staying with me?

Am [i] a hypocrite because [i] want both of us to work,
but [i] want to be the hog with the big nuts?
Am [i] a hypocrite because [i] want you to
forever look high school skinny while my belly can
continue to bloat and enlarge like European expansion?
Am [i] a hypocrite because [i] don't want children,
but [i] want you to have the operation?
[i] mean, you don't expect me to cash in my manhood,
do you?

Am [i] a hypocrite because [i] won't marry a woman
with a child, even though [i] have five of my own?
Am [i] a hypocrite because [i] want you to taste my juices,
but [i] won't kiss you any lower
than the equator of your umbilical cord?

Am [i] a hypocrite
because [i] want you to believe in my dreams,
but [i] want you to invest all of your seeds into my crops?
Am [i] a hypocrite because when [i] said "[i] do"
that meant you will every night of the week,
but once [i] get mine [i] can roll over
like a sack of potatoes and go to sleep.

Am [i] a hypocrite, or am [i] a man?
And if [i] am a hypocrite, what does that make you
for staying with me?

You talking 'bout call Tyrone; hell, you should have known
that [i] wasn't worth two pennies and an empty beer can
the first time [i] asked you for money.
But you were too busy looking at
my face, my body, my car, and my Mandingo.
You got this pretty ass wrapper,
and ain't nothing in the box.
All delusional dreams melt like cotton candy
in the hot mouth of reality.
[i] suggest next time,
before you take it home,
open the box.

To Joshua and Natasha

[i] wanted to marry your mother,
but the three of you were a packaged deal.
[i]'ve never wanted to plant or raise my own crops,
but [i] was addicted to the soil of your mother.
Her soul was a river where [i] could be baptized.
So, [i] said what the hell, in a few years it would be time
for y'all to harvest your independence,
fleeing the coop like recently freed slaves.
Then your mother and [i] could harvest our love in peace.
So, [i] acted like the step-father
like it was a step away from the real thing,
as if $20.00 and dropping you off at the mall
were the extent of my dadly duties.
Like Doug Williams in the game of your lives,
the two of you were never fazed.
In your quiet oak strength, you affirmed, "He'll learn."

It's amazing what days can do,
how weeks string and stream months into years.
In time, young swelling hearts and four tiny hands
can wear away the metal of the coldest wall,
until there are no longer any steps in the house,
and no one is any longer hyphenated.
You've given me a universe more
than [i]'ll ever give you.
You have been a birth experience
trampling down the Jericho Gate around my heart,
making me see the mirror of myself.
And though [i] still don't want to farm,
one hundred times have [i] flowered from knowing you.

Repentance: A Sinner's Prayer

A sinner on the edge of Hell's Eve,
to be baptized into his flesh, sees
the light on either end of the tunnel—
lost, he is a slave to the lava of his lust,
a puppet to his body.
His guilt and fear balled like intestines inside him,
like rock hard excrement,
squeezing, like a python, the life from him;
he hears voices mumbled in his brain.
He is their concubine.
Weak and trembling, his legs rubbery like Jell-O,
he falls to his knees and begs.

Deliver my soul, Lord.
Make me a special package that can be received.
Deliver my soul, Lord.
Rip from my bowels Satan's leeches.
[i] am homeless, Lord.
Deliver my soul, Lord.
You are my stewpot shelter.
Deliver my soul, Lord.
You are my double A twelve-step center
for [i] am drunk with sin.
[i] am sorry, Lord.
Make me regurgitate my life of filth, Lord.
Don't let me go through that one-way door, Lord.
Show me the golden knobs, Lord.
Deliver my soul, Lord.
[i] don't want to be a lock
on the door to someone else's salvation.
[i] surrender like the confederate that [i] am.
"All to you [i] freely give."
But, [i] want to be Reconstructed for the real Union.
Move my feet with your hands Jesus.
Explode your volcanic love all over me, Lord.
Let it rain on my dirty soul, Lord.
Impregnate me with your will, Lord.
Wash me like fresh laundry, Lord.

Remove the cataracts from my soul, Lord.
Shape the green brick of my mind, Lord.
[i] am a pitiful Peter frozen on the water.
[i]'ve looked into the mirror and have seen
the smiling face of Lucifer as my reflection.
Evaporate my moist hate and damp anger
with your glorious heat.
Massage my heart, Lord.
Spring clean the wretched and filthy house of my soul,
Lord.
Repaint the yellow streak that runs down my back, Lord.
Focus my dim and hazed eyes past the will of my flesh.
Make your love an enema to my constipated spirit.
Please Jesus, make me your poem.
Save me….Save *me*
Nobody but you Lord…
can make me sleep like a baby in his mother's bosom.

Hair Complex

My hair's vocabulary is wider than *Webster*'s
and deeper than the Nile, gut punching my people,
calling up molested memories of times
when Black was a voucher for slavery,
and we wore the hazy sunglasses of Hegel
as he echoed the sentiments of pale philosophers
that Africa has only been the world's sewer.
My hair, without a sound, resonates loudly like a
ringing weather alarm in the souls of onlookers,
"Pssst, remember when Black was monstrous?"
So, we got conks to straighten the naps of our history.
We assimilated to be accepted,
erasing ourselves with Revlon and Dark 'n Lovely.

But, you can't kill a good nap, just like man has no tools
to destroy structures built by the Truth
as rain, like baptism, reverses the effects of lies
calling us to the constant Truth of nappiology.

Time, the great History teacher,
revealed the Truth about the Earth's womb.
In finding our nappy ends, we found our sunshine
(some of us);
The hair we once straightened
we now wear the way God curled it,
affirming our relationship to the Big Black Continent,
our belief in beauty (some of us).
But the conk, like evil, won't die.
Here [i] am, a fossilized relic from the days
when Negroes feared Blackness like leprosy
'cause their bellies burned
with the shame of their cursed color
form having drunk the sperm of white supremacy.
And my hair, a Polaroid of poor fashion decisions,
speed dials all of those bad memories
that we are still trying to twist from our souls.

And still [i] process, eloped with TCB because

History was a neighbor [i] never visited.
It was only style, like changing clothes.
But for the sake of discourse,
why is straight fashionable and nappy not?
And before every conk, [i] flirt with the clippers.
But, [i] am an American African
whom the walls of television have made an isolationist
through his heavy-handed Euro-painted existence.
And the picture painted by hair
is not the same portrait that [i] see.
(A conking hero breeds conking flowers.)
And my hot hundred degree attitude of being an island
alienates me from my tribe,
([i] don't care that you stare)
especially since [i] pay my own rent.
Hair, damit!

The conk, like HIV, is interwoven into my system!!?!
[i]'m a self-loathing Black who hates whites!?!
[i]'m a chicken grease, café nigga with a degree!?!
[i]'m a walking fit of confusion…
Do you know where [i] stand…?

Exercise in Identity

Purple paisley generation, onyx male—
A big white foot steps in a brown ant bed,
pieces of Black marble recycled as flakes
in sallow stone—
WestAfroSouthernAmerican
existing in the Ivory Tower.
It's blowing chalky, suffocating pale covers on me
as blots of my creamy Black stick to it.
We are both grayed.
[i] continue to wander crookedly
through fields tilled in my crimson,
which have no place for me to breathe.
But it is this brightly stained path of
broken and bleeding marrow
that is my registration card to be.
And my knowledge of this
takes its callus stained, historical hands
and pushes me in my back toward my destiny.

Friendship

Unspoken words dance on the internet of our minds
manifest into action by the body's large lexicon.
Nods and glances, slight modifications in breathing
all having the most intricate articulations.
With the clearing of your throat,
water is at your fingertips before your mouth makes sound.
The roll of my neck draws your hands,
like magnets, to the muscles of my back.
A slight shiver under the covers,
and [i] turn up the thermostat.
Soul bearing breaks through the dams of pride and fear.
Weak and feeble words find comfort in your ear.
Subtle touches speak paragraphs to moments.
Friendship is in the secret vocabulary
of the eyes and breath.
It remains long after the pebble point of the argument
as been lost in the endless sands of months and years.
It's more resilient than leftover emotions
of a can-crushed ego or wounded eagle pride.
The body says [i]'m sorry before
the mouth can form the words.

Your friendship like the air leaving my lungs
is what will be missed most.
It was an anchor in an immense universe
of crumbling philosophies into a sea of disorder.

And in your going…
[i] thank you for once occupying the space of us.

My Lord's Prayer, 1998

My Father, living where [i] put you,
in some remote corner in the
general space of my cluttered mind
so that [i] am not held directly accountable to you,
whose name varies from individual to individual,
recognizing you in our own subjectively painted faces.
Upon whose Kingdom [i] await to reap
the benefits of my fleeting faithfulness
of aligning my will to as close to your will
as [i] Adamly can, given the fact that [i] was born of sin
while living on this Earth estranged from Heaven.
And to this day, give to me
my heart's desire, even though my
dumbbell inequities outweigh my
feather-light righteousness.
And forgive me of my weighty shortcomings
even though [i] am incapable of
forgiving my fellow man of his.
And lead me not to temptation
for [i] am not to be held accountable
for how my environment affects my actions,
causing me to perpetually fall further from you.
For all is yours
(the power, the glory, and the toys that [i] desire),
and [i] am only a piece in the monopoly board,
needing to be rescued and forgiven
as many times as there are pebbles on the beach
since, of course, you made me.
Amen.

Dreams, Visions and Epiphanies

> "Poems are like rainbows. They appear
> suddenly and leave us quickly"
>
> Langston Hughes

Dream Catcher

Sometimes, they wash down on me;
They are a flash rain on a shifting spring day,
they appear and vanish like God's etch-a-sketch,
leaving moist shadows of themselves.
[i] gather the drops in my little pots and buckets,
trying to catch enough to garner a cup of coherency.
[i]'m in a field of butterflies with no net.
The poet has a photographic memory;
the poet is a speed reader, soaking up and collecting,
squeezing out onto the grass of humanity.
But an imperfect vessel, my crossed and soiled eyes
disallow perfect replication or Xeroxing.
That's why the poet never wants those dream drops
to ever hit the ground. But, they do.
And the poet scoops dreams now soiled by earth's
experience, running over the combined, cupped hands,
trickling down the arm, gathering pieces of dirt and
perception along the way.
The poet scoops gallons and only drinks droplets, the rest
falling from the hands before the mouth sucks them in.
And sometimes the poet snatches the dreams
from the viscera of the sky, handling and managing clouds.
Performing C-section, the poet rips and shakes
the waters from the cloud's womb.
He is a bumbling god...who wakes and edits.
And sometimes dreams are regurgitated upon the poet
from the bowels of life.
The art is soaked within the smell of man's annals of Time.
The poet is a mirror of the soiled wetness and dried stench.
[i] am a dream catcher,
and [i] hurl those dreams against a blank canvas
so that you are baptized in a rainbow of opportunities.

Pieces and Moments of Heaven

Life, in the random showers of the sublime,
shows us what Heaven will be.
To keep your sanity uninfected,
you must experience seasonal booster shots.
Poor people trying to get a hook up for some,
while the rich trying to buy pieces of it.
But they both are trying to score
a touchdown in the ninth inning.
The trail to Heaven is buried in our personal soil
and will only flame up when ignited by
our lighter fluid actions.

This age of Artificial Nature
has removed us from the natural.
Man has lost his private line to God.
We can't caress God for our fellowship with the flesh.
We can't feel God through our concrete emotions.
We don't hear God over
the snap, crackle, and pop or ourselves.
We are empty frames, like abandoned shot gun houses,
and we fill ourselves with financed bullshit.

Heaven is the antonym of capitalism.
It's in a cool breeze on a Sunday morning before church,
two lovers snug in an old gown and worn pajamas,
standing on the back porch bathing
in an orange Mississippi October,
watching leaves fall and re-commune with the grass.
It's in a warm moment with a wife
on a chilly January evening after work,
hot coco, marshmallows, vanilla scented words,
soft and sliding caresses and gentle gliding kisses,
and a long night of mental consummation,
reading and talking 'til dawn
where words penetrate and impregnate us with glory.
Heaven is that beaming glow of knowledge
transmitted by the eyes and affirmed by the smile,
where all that matters is the still moment of now

and the only ramification is a spring of forever.

Pieces of Heaven are the flakes of our souls,
bits of agape which warms us
even in the darkest moments in Plato's cave—
the sharing of the last bite of a sandwich,
a forehead kiss on the way out the door,
and the moment our eyes say hello again.
Pieces of Heaven are smiles, touches, and hugs
that are as involuntary as spring rain
that soaks us to our nucleus.
Pieces of Heaven is the gathering up of God's love
keeping it in the flower pots of our hearts for
the coming dry tomorrows.

Regeneration: Life Keeps Giving Beauty

Flowers with green leaves deep enough to swim in, framed
by vibrating pink and yellow, explode from concrete.
In the alley, behind a store that sells fire juice,
sweet and tangy, milky chocolate, golden brown, and
caramel faces flash quick sun-beamed smiles between
soiled, stank laundromats where mean, faceless boys
use the pay phones to make transactions while chubby,
precious babies play barefoot in the parking lot.
The red and white Winston sign hovers o'er
the garbage can filled with cast aways' throw aways
as a young honor student passes the smell,
getting milk and eggs for his mother.
(The attendant follows him around the store.)
In the corner of the lot, five, six, and seven year old pigtails
play hopscotch in a chalked outline figure
with remnants of dried plasma from the weekend,
permanently tattooing the sidewalk as a record of decay.
Yet, it's their candy-coded childish game
that keeps us moving over the humps of humanity.
Later tonight under the cover of stars and gunshots
Li'l LeRoi will play security guard to his brothers and
sisters 'cause his mama has the night shift.
This is the plaster bond stronger than evil erosion.
He's passing on Love, the plasma of Life.
And as the mothers continue to fold clothes,
babies are roaming and moving, skirting and dashing
between their brick firm legs and pillow soft hips.
Subtle touches and short glances
speak volumes to little children.
Stop is the last spoken word
before the tanning of rear-ends.
Yet, before the tears have dried on the bouncy, chubby
cheeks, kisses on the forehead set it all back into motion.
And this play deserves a Tony
for its aesthetic achievement.
It's the script's subtleties and nuances of hope
which are the only reasons to keep waking up.

Ghetto Garden

Chalky crack residue and sullied,
damp condoms lead a trail between
toothpick thin, withered, decaying prostitutes and
rusted iron male statues,
as houses suffering from malnutrition
become eroding and leaning frames decorated
with cluttered, smashed old cans lay out
a path right up to the edges of the gritty, grainy soil.
The grayed film of hopelessness
dulls the Sun from the second-hand city.
An old man—a caramel skeleton in overalls—
walks this path, his arms nothing but rubbery veins,
used muscles, and screwdriver bones;
a thin body but sturdy from the steel of his fortitude
carries an earth-colored hoe
that has seen as many plantings as Moses.

The yearly revolution of spring puts him into motion.
First, the cutting of crabby grass and wayward weeds,
the removing of the remains of discarded lives:
a left shoe, three-fourths of a pair of pants,
worn car tires, something indefinable, a rag that has been
squeezed of his redness, and part of a hat—
what one finds in an abandoned ghetto time-capsule.
Layer by layer, he makes his earthly womb ready for
fertilizing, laying survival seeds of corn, greens, and beans
to sprout like a phoenix from the iron grave.

It's summer when a ghetto garden
emanates a magical miasma.
No one dares discard anything in that
green bed of reincarnation.
Pimps and gangsters tie their tongues in its presence,
and prostitutes walk a little more erect in passing.
This farmer receives more alter calls and hallelujahs
than the preachers or the police.
His gardens preach daily sermons
of Nature's will to crack the concrete cage

and be as bright as a July sun.
Crops pushing up the soil, finding the groove of sweet
survival even in the gutbucket blues of blacktop decay.

The tall corn raises its regal head
and sways with a swagger.
The greens, so full and round,
wiggle in the wind like a peacock.
And the green and orange tomatoes look like
an ever happening egotistical sunset.
The garden is a universe of exploding colors;
the gardener the master keeper of this rainbow of
possibilities, ordering his world at will,
this street corner Picasso, painting gold meaning and
diamond value to our ghetto existence.
In the middle of asphalt death,
the gardener finds the beat of Nature's heart
in a river of artichokes.

Looking upon this scene,
the concrete citizens escape into Nature's bosom,
realizing, if just for a moment, what it means to be ripe.

Revolution Is Born from Pain

Anger is the prodigal progeny of pain.
Revolution is the electrical fire of improperly installed
wires that burns when we have no more cheeks left to turn.
It's the pain of someone stabbing you with their razor sharp
fear of a shadow that you didn't know you were casting.
It's the pain of rejection even when you
didn't purchase the cruise ticket to come here.
It's the pain of being painted with the colors of
stained savagery, the indigo of ignorance, and the rusted
brown of heathenism when you've never walked one mile
to colonize anyone, when you were in your own living
room, minding your own business when colonization came
with its cold and greedy hands knocking on your front door
like an unwelcome teller marketer.

Anger, animosity, rage, and hate are merely the rashy,
runny sores and excrements of pain—
what pain will become if left infected too long.
These seething scabs are what happens when a hurting
people become tired of believing that it's actually rain
being urinated on them.

Revolution rises from the flames of pain.
Injustice is a sword that hurts before it bleeds.
Tears are the first retaliation.
The souls of Blacks flow from the ancient Nile Valley
where love runs abundantly like a river.
This is that spirit that courses in us.
But when pinned and restricted, the Nile will explode,
becoming Nat Turner's bloody roar through plantations,
like summer fires roaring through Yellow Stone.

This is our revolution. Caged pain with nowhere to go.

It is the pain of knowing a child
who is your mirror reflection will be denied education
because he's tattooed with your image.
It is the pain of being the prey of humanity's

greatest who-done-it hunt,
and having that novel reduced to
two paragraphs in an eleventh grade history book.
It is the pain caused when those whose hands are stained
with the blood of that crime wipe themselves clean on a
towel thrown under the rug of cleansed curriculums.
It's the pain of understanding that faces painted like yours
know they have a pass to whiteout the lives
of faces smeared with the same colors as you.
It's the pain of swallowing the liquid myth muddy waters
that infect your bowels with the virus of self hate.
It is the pain of being forced to live separate and unequal
and then being sent to jail for being separate and unequal.
It's it the pain of longer sentences
for cooking it instead of grinding it
or smoking it instead of snorting it.
It is the pain of having someone
clutch their purse in your presence after having
just worked the be-there-all-damn-day shift.
It is the pain of having a sales attendant become your
security shadow after having chopped cotton all summer
for some new school clothes.
It is the pain of having a four point GPA
and still needing firm action to gain access.
It is the pain of having the keys to no door.
It is the pain of loathing your image
because you do not realize that it is
the mirror that is cracked and stained.

This is the seed of revolution.
Revolution comes when once wet tear ducts become
flaming deserts, when the fearful have become
too anesthetized of life's cannons to be afraid,
when the weary are too tired to be weak.
This is when pain, like maggots from garbage,
mutates into its organic metamorphosis
and becomes sprouting rage, becomes revolution.
Revolution is a Phoenix bursting from a volcano of pain.
But there is never the need for the scalpel of revolution
without the impregnating of injustice into mankind's womb

My Psalm

The Lord is my Financial Advisor: [i] shall never be broke.
He delivereth me to a safe neighborhood: [i] can
      afford a level five schooling for my offspring.
He restoreth my assets: He leadeth me in the paths of
      prosperity for His name's sake.
Yea though [i] live in the times of a shaky market
      with an increasing FICA, [i] will fear no layoff,
      merger, or downsizing.
Thy annual returns and Thy net gains, they comfort me.
Thou preparest an IRA account and a 403(b) in the
      presence of my bill collectors: [i] am debt free:
Thou anointest my head with new tax laws;
      my bank account runneth over like the Mississippi
      River: [i] am paid.
Surely high yields and security shall follow me all the
      days of my life; and [i] will dwell in the economic
      institution of the Lord forever

The Lord is my Cadillac: [i] shall never walk.
He delivereth me from point A to point B: [i] never have to
      catch the bus or bum a ride.
He restoreth my mobility: He driveth me on the
      interstate of freedom for His name's sake.
      [i] am never late.
Yea though [i] drive through the bowels of the hood,
      [i] will fear no breakdown or no jacking; for
      [i] am safely locked within Him.
Thy 100,000 mile guarantee, Thy V8 engine,
      and Thy anti-lock breaking system comfort me.
When others scramble and pollute their clogged systems
      with oil, He cleanses my engine with nature's
      ethanol for a smoother ride that lasts as long as He
      provides grass or corn liquor; thus, my gas tank
      runneth over.
Thou anointest me with full-coverage insurance;
Surely safe driving and no tickets shall follow me all the
      days of my life, and [i] will dwell in the plush
      luxury ride of my Lord forever.

The Lord is my teacher: He sharpens my mind into
    a weapon of righteousness.
He maketh me to lie down in the bosom of His wisdom;
    He plants in my mind the seeds of scripture that
    bare fruit to a world staved for the nutrition of
    knowledge.
He restoreth my mind; He leads me in the paths of
    intelligence for His name's sake.
Yea though [i] walk through the era of cuts in educational
    spending, [i] fear no conservative. For Thou art
    my pell grant and my guaranteed loan;
The knowledge of the History Book written by Him and the
    universe plotted by His design comforts me in the
    curricular cradle of liberal sciences.
Thou preparest a scholarship for me in the presence of the
    ending of Affirmative Action; Thou anointest my
    head with Washington, DuBois, Garvey, and
    Hughes; my brain runneth over like the financial aid
    line.
Surely A's, research grants, fellowships, Black owned
    businesses, and good government jobs will follow
    me all the days of my life, and [i] will dwell in the
    ivory tower of the Lord forever.

The Lord is my Poet; [i] shall not want.
He maketh me to be baptized in the fertile soil of his mind:
    He leadeth me to where fantasy impregnates
    reality, and we blossom into our utopian selves.
He restoreth my soul; He leadeth me in the paths of
    creativity and idealism for His name's sake.
Yea though [i] walk through the valley of petrified logic
    and pragmatism, [i] fear no critique; for His
    ingenious balm is with me; Thy images and
    metaphors comfort me.
Thou preparest a fulfilled existence for me in the presence
    of those with no dreams. Thou anointest my head
    with visions and epiphanies; my canvas is full.
Surely euphoria of the heart and mountain-moving art will
    follow me all the days of my life, and [i] will
    dwell in the imagination of my Lord forever.

www.ingramcontent.com/pod-product-compliance
Lightning Source LLC
Chambersburg PA
CBHW032148040426
42449CB00005B/438